FOREX TRADING STRATEGIES

Better Strategies to Increase Gains and Reduce Losses

The following book is reproduced below with the goal of providing information that is as accurate and reliable as possible. Regardless, purchasing this book can be seen as consent to the fact that both the publisher and the author of this book are in no way experts on the topics discussed within and that any recommendations or suggestions that are made herein are for entertainment purposes only. Professionals should be consulted as needed prior to undertaking any of the action endorsed herein.

This declaration is deemed fair and valid by both the American Bar Association and the Committee of Publishers Association and is legally binding throughout the United States.

Furthermore, the transmission, duplication or reproduction of any of the following work including specific information will be considered an illegal act irrespective of if it is done electronically or in print. This extends to creating a secondary or tertiary copy of the work or a recorded copy and is only allowed with an expressed written consent from the Publisher. All additional rights reserved.

The information in the following pages is broadly considered to be a truthful and accurate account of facts and as such any inattention, use or misuse of the information in question by the reader will render any resulting actions solely under their purview. There are no scenarios in which the publisher or the original author of this work can be in any fashion deemed liable for any hardship or damages that may befall them after undertaking information described herein.

Additionally, the information in the following pages is intended only for informational purposes and should thus be thought of as universal. As befitting its nature, it is presented without assurance regarding its prolonged validity or interim quality. Trademarks that are mentioned are done without written consent and can in no way be considered an endorsement from the trademark holder.

Table of Contents

Introduction 1

Chapter 1: Best Forex Trading Entry Strategies 3

Chapter 2: Best Forex Trading Stop Loss Strategies 9

Chapter 3: Best Forex Trading Take Profit Strategies 19

Chapter 4: Planning Trades Before Market Entry 25

Chapter 5: The Essential Steps of Profitable Trading 37

Chapter 6: Tips for Successful Forex Trading 47

Conclusion 55

Introduction

Congratulations on purchasing this book and thank you for doing so.

The following chapters will discuss some of the most crucial aspects of Forex trading. If you wish to become a successful Forex trader, then you need to learn a little more about how to minimize your losses and increase your gains.

To be successful as a Forex trader, you need to understand how to enter a trade, how to stop losses, and how to take profits and exit. These are some of the most important factors, and they are discussed in great detail in this book.

Far too many traders apply their technical knowledge and trading skills and actually win plenty of trades. However, they do not know how to exit thereby losing their hard-earned profits. This book teaches you how to exit trades and take profits at the right moment.

Traders also need to learn to be disciplined enough to stick with a strategy to the end. All too often, traders panic and quit a trade due to worry or concern. Such an approach will never earn you money. By reading this book, you will learn how to avoid emotions when trading and many other great tips for successful trading. You will also learn how to create wealth trading Forex for a long time to come.

There are plenty of books on this subject on the market, thanks again for choosing this one! Every effort was made to ensure it is full of as much useful information as possible, please enjoy!

Chapter 1
Best Forex Trading Entry Strategies

Trade entries are a huge determinant of whether your trades will be successful or not. Most traders tend to take entry points for granted and focus their energies on the actual trade. A shift from this approach towards application of the best trade entry strategies will significantly improve the risk-reward potential of any trade and also helps you to achieve a superior stop loss location.

As a trader, one of the most essential aspects you need to focus on is establishing if there is a trend in the market or not. Ordinarily, you would simply need to trade with the trend setup or consider setting up a countertrend reversal setup.

It is crucial that you learn how to determine the best Forex entry methods and the essential tools you require for market entry. There are a couple of different methods that you can use to successfully enter the market. If practiced consistently, they will enable you to become a more proficient trader.

1. Assess the Market

As a Forex trader, you really need to be able to recognize the environment in which the market is operating. By finding out the operating environment, you will then be able to establish the most appropriate strategies and tactics at any given time. You need to determine what kind of market structure you would like to trade and what type of trades you wish to make.

2. Scan your Charts

Among the first things you need to do before the start of your trading day is to scan your charts. You should first determine the best Forex pairs to trade then scan the charts. One of the best approaches is to scan the markets right after the closure of New York and the opening of European markets. During these hours, the market action goes down after the previous trading day.

Even as you scan the charts, be on the lookout for price action, levels, and trends. It is important to look out for a trend. For instance, watch out for any patterns that involve low highs and low lows or higher highs and higher lows. Also be on the lookout for the direction of the 21 and 8 daily EMAs.

3. Establish a Trend

You should endeavor to establish a trend. It all comes down to looking for the higher highs and higher lows versus the lower lows and lower highs. If you can establish a crystal clear trend, then it will be worth much more than gold. Successful traders always trade along with a trend and rarely against it.

4. Try and Set Up Trades at the End of Each Day

This is a very easy yet very effective approach. If you can set up your trade at the close of New York markets, then you will have an effective start. You will also eliminate any mental confusion and noise brought on by use of intraday charts. You should ensure that you monitor all your trades once or twice each trading day in order not to unnecessarily fiddle with the trades. This will also help to eliminate the psychological aspect of trading.

As a trader, you either specialize in one type of trading or are a master in several types and can choose a preferred type depending on market situation. It is important to keep this in mind when building your strategy. For a trader who has mastered different trading styles, the best approach is to focus on only a few currencies while a specialized trader should focus on scanning the market and viewing more Forex currency pairs.

Scanning the Market

When scanning the markets, the aim is to look for the following;

- Price action
- Trends
- Levels

What you need to determine first is whether there is a trend in the market. This is ideally not science but actually an art. Patterns of high highs and low lows are crucial at this stage because they point to a trend.

Get Better Prices with Limiting Orders

A limiting order is also known as a pending order. It is placed above or below the prevailing market price depending on the direction of the trade. Limiting orders provide you with the ability to enter a trade at a price of your choosing. The only challenge is that you may not always get into a trade at all.

If you are trading short, the limiting order should be set just above the prevailing market price. However, if you are trading long, then the limiting order should be placed below the prevailing market price. Here is how to apply the limiting order.

1. The Trade Entry Tip: This is simply where a trader enters a price action signal on a 50% retrace. It simply means that you enter a limited order where the price retraces back to the 50% level of a pin bar. This approach greatly improves your risk vs. reward ratio, and it allows you to place a tighter stop loss. You will easily be able to double your returns.

Another benefit of this approach is that you have more flexibility regarding where it is that you place or locate your stop loss. You can choose the normal distance stop loss or enter a trade with a much tighter stop loss. You get more breathing space within your trades as a trader when you use a regular stop loss distance using a limit entry order on a pin bar. Limit orders enable you to attract the market your way because you only enter a trade if it moves towards your preferred price. There are chances of missing out on the trade simply because the price may not necessarily reach your preferred level. However, it is much better to use this approach because of the flexibility it offers.

2. Daily chart time frame: This chart time frame is a lot more relevant to setting out your entry points than you may be aware. This is because it is more useful than other charts with low time frames. The daily chart can be considered to be a natural filter for any bad entries. It actually filters out irrelevant and outstanding price movement of the lower time frame. Because of this, the daily chart signals become a lot more reliable.

Essential Tools for Market Entry

1. For the level pickers

Fibonacci retracement, trendline bounce, chart pattern bounce, bottom and top of range, the highs and lows, the top and bottom, and the Fibonacci target.

2. For the momentum breakout traders

Chart pattern breaks, break of the bottom or top, the trend line breaks, a fractal indicator break, and a break of the low or high.

3. For confirmation traders

Tools such as indicator confirmations, fractal break in anticipated direction, and candlestick formations in regions where support and resistance are expected.

Trade Style and Psychology

Generally, traders will have a preference of an entry strategy. This preference will depend on the trading psychology and style. Some traders prefer to wait for a momentum break and cannot handle early entries. Others prefer to trade a pullback as these enable them to plan early. The trading psychology and style are crucial factors that often influence the entry strategy.

Chapter 2

Best Forex Trading Stop Loss Strategies

It is almost impossible for any trader to survive the Forex markets without a reasonable risk management strategy. A stop-loss strategy is one of the most important risk management strategies available to traders. Learning about the crucial stop loss strategies is absolutely essential.

The good news is that with stop loss orders, you will easily be able to protect your trades from negative emotions like fear and greed. If unchecked, such emotions can cause havoc to your trades.

What is a Stop Loss Order?

A stop-loss order is simply any order that you place so that a security that you hold is sold when a certain price is achieved. The order is usually placed with your Forex broker. Such an order is created to minimize the losses a trader might incur after taking a position. It is absolutely imperative to institute stop loss orders any time a trade is initiated.

There are a couple of ways that such an order can be implemented. This is why it is important to actually come up with a good strategy that will suit a particular trade, market, or situation.

1. The Initial Stop Loss Placement

This particular stop loss strategy largely depends on the trading strategy that you choose. While some personal preferences can come into play, it is one that is definitely common with many Forex traders.

If you adopt the pin bar trading strategy, then the stop loss can be placed directly behind the tail end of the pin bar. This move applied to both the bearish and bullish pin bars.

With the inside bar trading strategy, you should place the stop loss either behind the inside bar's low or high or behind the mother bar's low or high. In both these cases, should the price hit the stop loss, they strategies become invalid, and this simply means the set up was not sufficiently strong.

2. The Hands Off Stop Loss Strategy

Another excellent stop-loss option that you can apply is the "Set and Forget" strategy which is also known as the "Hands Off" strategy. The aim of this strategy is very simple. As a trader simply set your stop loss strategy and just let the market run its course. It alleviates any chance of getting stopped way too soon as the stop loss is maintained at a relatively safe distance.

This strategy doesn't involve your hands so that you do not have to do anything once it is set up. The aim here is to ensure there is no temptation to make adjustments to the stop loss as you trade. There are some obvious advantages of using this particular method. These are listed below.

- Keeps emotional trading under control
- Eliminates the chance of getting stopped too early
- Frees up the trader, so they focus on trades
- It is a very simple policy to implement

This kind of approach helps to reduce chances that a trade will be stopped too early by ensuring the stop loss is placed at a far enough distance. As traders, we know the challenges of moving the stop loss too early as our trades are stopped only to see the markets proceed in the correct direction.

It is imperative that emotions are eliminated from your trades. This way, reason will prevail, and you will be successful in your trades thanks to this stop-loss measure. All you do once you set up the stop loss is to simply sit back and let the market take its course. Also, this stop-loss method is simple to implement because it is only handled once. Then as soon as it is set up, you can forget about it.

However, there are some disadvantages or downside of this particular set up measure. These are recounted below.

- Traders are often tempted to move the stop loss closer to entry point
- High risk because traders stand to lose the maximum possible amount

A trader who puts $500 on a trade stands to lose this amount as it is also the maximum possible amount that can be lost. This is risky and should, therefore, be approached with caution.

Sometimes traders feel the temptation to move the stop loss from where it is to where they feel safer. The Forex market is wrought with temptations, and a disciplined trader should learn to fend off such temptations.

3. Break Even Stop Loss Measure

Yet another useful and applicable stop-loss measure that we can institute is the break-even strategy. Lessons on stop-loss strategies are incomplete without this particular method. Traders often adopt this measure to protect their capital. Traders feel safe that they cannot lose money using this stop-loss strategy.

Often, you will find traders moving their stop loss close to the entry price. This is not a bad strategy, but at least it protects you as a trader. Here are some of the benefits of this strategy.

- You do not need to conduct market analysis with this strategy
- It is a very simple strategy to implement
- It gets rid of any imminent risk of a given trade

Once this strategy is in place, any risk to the trade is eliminated. Any market movements will then be protected by your stop loss measure, keeping you safe as the market plays out. Also, you will not need to conduct any complex, or simple, market analysis.

Simply determine your entry point and use it to determine your stop loss.

The break-even stop-loss strategy is also one of the easiest strategies to implement. It is always easy to know where to place the stop loss no matter the trade. Even then, this measure has some disadvantages.

- This strategy hinders your odds
- It makes use of an arbitrary level which is not the best approach
- It puts traders at risk of emotional trading

Because the only determinant of the stop loss measure depends on your entry point and not market analysis, then this is an arbitrary approach. Such an approach does not portend much success compared to others.

This strategy will limit most likely limit your chances of success because it does not give any of your trades a chance to be successful. There is not enough room to move and maneuver. This is in contrast to the price action confluence that should essentially give you better odds. However, this stop-loss strategy does allow the price action confluence to be in your favor and therefore affects your odds.

4. The 50% Stop Loss Strategy

This is a strategy that aims at cutting your risks by 50%. However, it does not necessarily cut your risks by exactly half. The main benefit of applying this strategy is that it makes use of the markets and enables traders to understand how much of their capital they need to protect.

Basically, if you apply this strategy and enter the market based on the daily close, the market may close slightly higher the following day. Now you can choose the day's low to determine your stop-loss measure. Now, when the markets close the following day after your entry, you can use the low of that day to determine the stop-loss point. This way, you will cut your risk by half. What this simply states is that should the market go below the previous day's low, then you will not proceed with the trade. There are some outright advantages of this kind of set up.

- Allows the use of the price action level
- Will cut your risk by up to 50%
- Gives your trades sufficient room to breathe

Cutting your risk by half is beneficial and actually good for your trades. For instance, if one of your trades was worth $100, then you could easily ensure that you lose no more than 50% on this trade.

This strategy makes use of the price action level. Due to this, it is unlikely that the market will get to the stop loss. In this instance, the market lows and highs are in play and hence the stop is protected. This is a much better approach as compared to other strategies such as the break even stop loss strategy.

Also, this system allows the market space to breath. This means trades can freely occur without a trader having to exit. Market movements are essential if you are to make money trading Forex currencies. However, there are some downsides to this strategy. For instance;

- There is still the possibility of stopping trades prematurely
- Trades are still at 50% risk of loss

Although this strategy allows your trades to get some much-needed breathing space, the trades are at risk of being stopped prematurely. This fact is particularly true for trades that involve currency pairs with volatile price action. Also, your trades will be at a 50% risk of losing out. This can be acceptable for some trades but unacceptable to others.

You can use market conditions during trade to determine whether the 50% stop loss strategy is the most suitable for your purpose. Take for example a situation where the market closed very close to the previous day's low. Then in such a situation, the 50% strategy would not work because it would have to be too close to the prevailing market rates.

Monitor your Stop Loss

When the market starts to move in a direction that favors you, then you should consider trailing your stop loss. Trailing the stop loss when the market is trending in your direction will help you protect your trading capital. It is important to note that a stop loss can be monitored either automatically or manually. Most modern trading platforms offer traders this option so they can choose if they wish to trail the stop loss or not.

The automated one is generally managed by the system so you will not necessarily need to worry about it. However, when manually following it, you will need to use price action levels to determine the trailing point of the stop loss.

Example

Take for example a trade situation where you purchase the Euro USD at 1.35. You can set the trailing stop loss at approximately 50 pips. Assume that the market actually moves in your favor and you gain up to 1.39 and this move gains you 400 pips. The stop loss will now adjust to 1.355.

It is therefore essential that you trail the stop loss marker manually, whenever possible, using indicators such as the price action levels. This way, you will remain safe and will use reliable indicators that give you more room to maneuver and allow trades to prosper.

It is absolutely critical that you use stop loss strategies as a Forex trader. There are a couple of strategies available so you will need to determine which is the most appropriate for each trade. For this, you will need to master how to use confluence to your advantage, how to use the best risk-reward ratio and how to define price action strategies and determining key levels.

Importance of Setting a Small Short Order

You need to set small short orders for some reasons. For starters, such short orders help to protect you from losses. This is essentially why it is so named. You trade to make money and not lose it. A small short order achieves this effectively.

The first and most important benefit of using a small short order is that it limits the losses to within acceptable margins. This is important because it protects your capital and limits exposure.

You can also effectively use it to lock in profits. This is why a short order is sometimes referred to as a trailing order. Locking in profits is crucial for Forex traders because profit is the main reason why we trade.

The short stop-loss order also helps eliminate emotion from a trade. When feelings get involved, and a trader uses emotions, then his trade will most likely fail, and he will lose money.

Some traders do not use stop loss measures and instead allow a losing trade to run hoping the market will run and turn the trade around. This is a wrong approach that could cost you money and affect your trading capital. You should instead use a stop loss placement to mitigate losses.

CHAPTER 3
Best Forex Trading Take Profit Strategies

It is a fact that every trader trades to realize a profit and make money. This could be either primary income or additional income, but the fact is traders do it for the sake of profits.

All traders in the Forex markets have their own trading strategies. However, at the end of the trading day, they need to make money. It can be disastrous for a trader to spend precious hours trading the markets only to see their profits disappear simply because they did not know where to exit. Being able to identify the most appropriate exit points is crucial for successful trading in the Forex markets.

Even the best or most experienced traders need to have effective profit taking strategies otherwise they will lose money and become ineffective traders. Therefore, as a trader, once you are in a trade, your work is not yet done. Rather, it has only just begun. Trade management and exit plans need to be implemented and not overlooked. They are a huge part of trading but, sadly, are often overlooked by many traders. Most of the time the aim is to get out close to the top, but actually, the main objective is to make money. Here is a look at some of the most popular take profit strategies used by successful Forex traders.

Importance of Trade Exits

According to experts, trade management and exits are the most crucial factors of any Forex trade. They are even more important that the entry strategies. However, and surprisingly, not many traders pay attention to the management and exit strategies. Yet exits can make or break a trade strategy.

According to research by trade experts and writers, no two traders approach trades the same way even under similar conditions. In most cases, the trader with the best trade management and exit skills will emerge the winner. Those without proper exit strategies may even incur losses.

Trade performance depends on a couple of factors that including trade management, limiting losses, and profit-taking techniques. However, applying these techniques is not as easy as it sounds and many traders often fair poorly in this regard.

There are plenty of reasons why many trades are not profitable. Here is a look at some of these reasons.

- Watching a price move only to see it reverse direction before taking profits

- Exiting a position at an average price due to price retracement

- Traders sometimes move a stop loss, and they opt to break even too soon

- Placing the take profit position close to the open price halfway in a trade

- Closing a trade too early and denying the take profit position to be attained

- Missing a market reversal and then losing all profits accrued

As traders, our instincts are always to grab a profit whenever the chance presents itself. This is natural and very common as we avoid losing the profit. However, this is never advisable. It is important to resist the temptation of taking profits early and learn to let the trade run its course. Delayed gratification, in this case, is way more profitable compared to instant gratification.

As a Forex trader, you really should learn patience and practice it as you trade. Also, you need to learn to stick to your original plan. All too often, traders change their minds and divert from the original plan. You will get much better results if you stick with the trade and initial plan.

1. Ensure that you Ride Winners Adequately

There is a saying about assurances in any trade. Basically, there are only two certainties that can occur. As a trader, you will have winning trades, and you will also have losing trades. To be a successful trader, you will have to learn to ride the winning trades adequately.

To be a successful trader, you should ensure that you fund your ongoing successful trades to make even larger profits. Let us assume that, as a trader, you have done your due diligence such as use technical analysis. If this analysis indicates that a winning trade still has some way to go, then you can pump in more funds into this trade so that you earn a much bigger profit.

Many professional traders often say that the success of their trades lies largely in riding on winning trades. There are a couple of ways to ride on a winning trade. One of the most popular ways of doing this is applying the pyramid process. This process simply means pouring in more money onto the winning trade with the hope of maximizing profits. Here is how the approach works.

- Let us assume the initial trade is allocated at $15000
- The risk on this trade is put at $300
- A second position is then added as soon as the first gets to breakeven
- This second position should mirror the first one so add $15000
- This second trade rises and nears resistance
- You can have another pyramid at 60% so add $9000
- As soon as the resistance point is attained, take profit and exit

You will notice that you earn a lot more profit with this approach compared to letting it proceed to profit level. This is, therefore, an extremely useful tip that you can apply to earn significantly more money.

As you trade, there are some important aspects that you need to focus on. For instance, try and ensure that your stop loss' initial position is either at breakeven point or better. Ensure that the system where you are trading essentially has the potential to get the solid trending moves. But there is no need of using this approach if the risk-reward ratio is about 1:1.

2. Make Large Profits with Minimal Losses

The adage among traders is to let a winning run continue but exit any losing trades. However, applying this adage is not that easy for traders. This is because when faced with large profits, the instinct is often to lock them in. However, this is not the ideal approach of this particular strategy.

This strategy basically insinuates holding onto a winning position and hanging in there, so the profits keep rising. Patience is a requirement for the success of this strategy. Anytime that a trade is heading your way and performing as well or better than expected, then profits will be on the rise. At such a time, you should not be packing and exiting the trade but rather hang in there, hold your nerve, and ensure you profit from the run as much as possible.

Like earlier pointed out, some of the wealthiest and most successful Forex traders are those who capitalized on profitable runs. A lot of the time, traders also need to learn to run away from losing trades. It is said that the first cut is the cheapest which loosely means that exiting a losing trade is beneficial if done quickly. The sooner you exit a losing trader, the less money you lose. This will prevent you from suffering larger and more painful losses.

3. You Can Take Your Money and Start Afresh

As a trader, you still have the option of exiting a trade and starting all over again. This strategy is more applicable to short-term active traders such as day traders. The main aim here is to collect sufficient profits from a successful trade within a certain period.

Such a strategy does make sense especially to traders who wish to avoid taking risks with overnight trades.

Basically, situations change and overnight movements could wipe out any accrued profits. Taking profits within a trade and then closing the position and exiting the trade gives you a chance to start all over again and repeat the process. A lot of active day traders actively pursue this strategy.

There are ideally only two different ways of taking advantage of this profit taking Forex strategy. One is to apply a dollar or percentage profit target. Therefore, you can work out a suitable percentage for any given trade where you will take profits. As soon as the set percentage or dollar amount is attained, you should exit the trade and possibly start a new one. For instance, if you have a dollar amount target of about $500, you will trade until the amount is attained. Once attained, you should exit and then plan on the next trade.

Some traders use technical analysis to determine or guide their trades. Such traders often opt for technical profit levels. They often work with indicators such as the Fibonacci levels, support and resistance levels and so on. It is a great idea to consider using technical levels or indicators that can easily be used on any MT4 chart. This way, you will have an easy and clear indication of when to exit or stay in a trade.

Chapter 4
Planning Trades Before Market Entry

Building a trading plan is by far the single most important aspect of your success as a Forex trader. You absolutely have to take time and plan your trades from start to conclusion. All too often traders will enter a trade without a clear plan or vision. They believe that a particular trade is a winning one and they fear losing out. Such traders jump into a trade and start making a profit. However, once the tide turns, they turn around and try again. This will lead to huge losses and profitability might be missed simply because there was no pre-trade planning.

It is crucial that you treat trading as a business and not a side gig or hobby. This way, you will take it more seriously and will have a better chance of success. If you have no idea what a trading plan or how it looks like, then it is better to learn as it is among the most crucial aspect of your trading life and success.

Forex Trading Considerations

As a trader, you need to understand that the key to success is actually emotional discipline and not intelligence. If the main ingredient were intelligence, then there would be a lot more people out there trading and making money.

Motivation

Even before you begin trading, think about the reasons why you are a Forex trader? What are your desires, ambitions, or aspirations?

Are you seeking financial freedom or to be your own boss? Do you want to establish an additional source of income? Once you answer these questions, then you will be able to determine your motivation. It is this motivation that will keep you going from day to day, month to month and even for years to come. You need to keep in mind that trading Forex can be a fulltime job and is never a gamble. You can actually make money.

Have Realistic Trading Goals

As a trader, you need to think realistically about your goals and how you will go about achieving them. For instance, you cannot, as a trader, expect to earn a living trading Forex with an initial of $50, $500, or even $2000. With goals that are realistic, you will be able to set targets and meet them, feel motivated and keep going. Realistic goals also enable you to abide by risk management and money management rules. Here are some realistic goals that you can set for yourself.

- Always have a trade strategy
- Trade according to your strategy
- Be consistently profitable after 12 months
- Ensure capital growth by 3% each month

What type of trader are you?

You need to determine what type of trader you are. There are different kinds of Forex traders. The type of trader you aspire to be is mostly related to your persona as well as the time you have to dedicate to your trades. Forex trading essentially occurs in timeframes. You need to determine the trading timeframe that suits you best. Here is a look at the different types of traders.

1. Scalper:

A scalper is basically a trader who prefers trading the lowest timeframes. Such traders do not want to wait for long hours for their trades. They enjoy speedy setups and enjoy a lot of time with the charts each day. A scalper searches for the lowest spreads within a currency pair and often opts for the business times of the day for any major Forex currency pairs.

2. Day Trader

Most Forex traders are day traders. And many aspiring traders often envision themselves as day traders. Such traders don't enjoy scalping, and they consider it to be nerve-wracking. They are also not happy leaving trades open for lengthy periods of time. Day traders have plenty of time in their hands throughout the day and can spare moments to find trade setups and keep observing and monitoring them throughout the day. A day job is basically

3. Position Trader

A position trader is a Forex trader that enters a trade then finds and holds a position for a long while. This could be for weeks at a time and sometimes even for months. Therefore, they always base their trades, decisions, and moves on the fundamentals of a currency rather than technical analysis like other traders do. Such a trader needs to be very patient and must be able to predict the activity of the market within a month or longer. Such traders work with large stop losses mostly because of big market swings. They also need substantial capital amounts to effect their trades.

4. Swing Traders

A swing trader is a Forex trader who is happy to leave his or her trades open for a couple of days. Such a trader generally follows market swings in the correct direction. Swing trades often plan their trades intricately and prefer to focus on only a couple of trades at a time. These particular types of trades are suitable for people who do not have much time for their trades but are patient and willing to wait for lengthy periods of time for their trades to work right. Patience is a virtue for swing traders so keep that in mind. They also need to be disciplined enough not to exit a trade should the market move against them. An impatient trader would feel compelled to intervene, stop a trade, and possibly start a new one.

Determine the Kind of Trader you are

Part of your trading plan needs to contain your preferred type of Forex trade. When you eventually make the decision, make sure to write it down as part of your larger trading plan.

There are a couple of things that will basically determine the kind of trader you are going to eventually become. These include your trading strategy. Ideally, your trading strategy should define a couple of things including how you plan, select, open, manage, and eventually exit a trade. It is very likely that you have an idea of how you accomplish each step, but it needs to be written down as part of your strategy. For instance, how do you choose your trades? What are the determining factors or essential ingredients?

Here are some of the essential ingredients that constitute a good trading strategy.

- Do you have a trading setup? Your trading setup should include things such as technical and fundamental indicators as well as trading timeframe.

- Do you have any established rules?

- Are there any exit tools?

- How are stop loss and take profit strategies determined?

- Will you use a trailing stop?

- Are there conditions that would compel you to quit a trade early?

What about Risk Management?

One of the most essential aspects of Forex trade and trading, in general, is risk management. This refers to the percentage of your trading capital that you are willing to risk in any trade. It also points to the risk: reward ratio. As a trader, you may be wondering how much of your capital you should be willing to risk. The answer basically should be not more than 2%. Therefore, anytime you want to come up with a trading strategy, always think about risk management. Risk management is always considered using the risk: reward ratio or the 2% maximum risk allowed.

Always Keep a Trading Journal

Another important aspect of trade planning is keeping or maintaining a trade journal. A trading journal is simply a logbook where you record all your trades. You should endeavor to make this as routine as possible. This is an excellent way of turning you into a profitable trader within a very short period. A journal allows you to take and record notes so that you note what great things happen and any lessons that need to be learned. It is important to keep a trading journal because;

- It allows you to record notes of your emotions and sentiments while trading. For instance, if you thought you were losing but ended up winning, then you should not this down.

- A journal provides a reliable record of all your activity. This historic record enables you to conduct an analysis of previous trades so that you can determine what you did well and where you went wrong.

- It also enables you to confirm whether or not you followed the trading strategy that you had set out for yourself. If there were any discrepancies or failures, then these will become visible to you.

Summary of a Good Trading Plan

Here is a summary of the proper steps you need to take to come up with a suitable trading plan.

- Take into consideration your motivation for Forex trade
- Work within realistic goals so that you attain them
- Discover the kind of trader that you are
- Use a template to write down your trading plan
- Always have a risk management plan
- Ensure that you keep a trading journal

How to Make a Reliable Trading Plan

We have already determined that a Forex trading plan is essential for a successful trading strategy. Any plan that you come up with should be written in stone which means it should not change. However, it can be subjected to a review once the trading day is over or after the market has closed. Your plan can be adjusted as market conditions change and changed as your skills get better. Avoid using someone else's plan and come up with your own.

Assess your skill set

You need to determine whether you are ready to trade or not. If you have a system, then you should test it until you have confidence that it works. You need to be like the professionals who trade the markets confidently. They move in and take profits from traders who have no plans and keep making expensive errors.

Have a checklist and a routine

Any good trading plan should consist of a routine in trading activities. It is important to have a pre-determined routine so that you do not end up running around confused and out of focus. With the routine, you will also need discipline. Also, you should choose the most obvious market setups whenever you can so that you pick up any easy trades. You can, in fact, formulate your entire trading plan and make it a checklist. Having a smooth format that enables you to determine if a trade setup is worth it is absolutely important.

Trade Preparation

Make sure that you carefully determine the program and trading system that you will use. If you intend to use signals, then ensure that these are easily visible and can be detected clearly with a clear auditory or visual signal.

Come up with clear exit rules

A lot of traders often focus more on finding buy signals. 90% of their attention is spent looking for entry points and so on. However, they pay very little attention to the appropriate points of exit. Often, traders will not sell when they are down as they are unwilling to take a loss. To make it as a successful trader, you will need to overcome such concerns. A lot of professional traders lose more trades than they win but because of their money management and exit rules, they still end up making a profit.

Therefore, always find out your exit points before you enter a trade. Each trade has at least two exit points. Write down your stop loss points and do not count on mental notes. Also, ensure that each trade has a profit target. Once you hit this target, you should collect some of your profits and then move your stop loss position to break even. Also, do not risk losing more than the percentage that you initially set.

Prepare yourself mentally

It is extremely important that you prepare yourself for the day ahead. You will need a clear head and focus. A good trader always has to be up to the challenge. Experienced traders will tell you that it is better to take the day off and not trade at all if you are psychologically and emotionally unprepared. Otherwise, you will simply not be able to participate fully in any trade and you will not only lose huge amounts of money but will worsen your mental situation.

It is easy to be mentally unprepared when you are angry, distracted, or preoccupied with other thoughts. As a trader, you may want to have a mantra that you repeat regularly, probably once each day. Such a mantra should put you mentally at ease and into the trading zone. Also, avoid distractions within your trading area. Trading is business and distractions can cost you in a huge way.

Do your homework and due diligence

It is important that every morning, just before your trades begin, you should become acquainted with the goings on around the world. What is the situation in the markets? Are overseas markets up or down? Is there any company about to release its earnings report? Most traders prefer to wait for the release of such reports before making any major moves. This is a much better approach than taking unnecessary risks. You can use index futures to gauge the mood of the market right before the markets open.

Come up with clear entry rules

Just like with the exit, you need to define and set clear entry rules. These rules will define how you enter a particular trade. It could be something like; if I have a signal B which fires and indicators show minimum target about 3 times larger than the stop loss and I am at support, then purchase Y contracts or X shares.

The system you use needs to be sufficiently complex to handle instructions effectively yet flexible enough to manage any snap decisions. For instance, if you have a total of 15 conditions that need to be fulfilled while most are subjective, then it may be challenging if not impossible to actually trade. It is worth noting that computers make much better traders compared to humans.

This is probably the reason why half of all trades on the New York Stock Exchange are executed by computer software and not people. Computers carry no emotions when trading. They simply follow a program set by a trader. When conditions are met, then they enter a trade. Should the trade proceed in the wrong direction, then they exit. But should a trade become profitable then the computer will take profits and exit. All decisions are based on probabilities and devoid of emotions and irrational thinking.

Post-trade post-mortem

It is advisable to conduct a post-mortem of each trade. While adding up the profits and working out any losses is important, understanding why is ten times more important. Have a trading journal where you write all your conclusions so that you learn, improve, and remember.

Conclusion

It is important to gain sufficient skill before embarking on Forex trading. There is never a guarantee that any trade will make money. However, your chances as a trader will improve drastically if you are sufficiently skilled and have a system that can assist you to win. All professional traders choose trades where the odds favor them. Otherwise, they wouldn't trade. However, during trades, they allow their profits to ride a winning trade and cut their losses short. This can result in some losses, but they will emerge winners overall.

Many traders who do not make money often do not trade the way that the pros do but instead do the exact opposite. Learning and improving skills should be one of your hallmarks. Also, as a trader, you need to treat your Forex trading as a fulltime job, part-time job, or a business. It is never a gamble or a game where you depend on luck. This way, you will take it seriously enough and aim to make rather than lose money. While no trade is ever guaranteed, it is crucial that you have a suitable plan so that you have much better chances of winning and making a consistent profit.

CHAPTER 5

The Essential Steps of Profitable Trading

Forex traders, especially beginners, need to learn about the steps necessary for profitable trading. Achieving long-term success trading profitably is a dream that many have, but only a few can achieve. Fortunately, there are steps that you can take that will ensure you become a successful, long-term, profitable trader. Here is a look at some of the essential steps that will lead you to successful trades.

1. Choose the Right Broker

When you feel totally ready to begin trading Forex currencies, then you should first embark on identifying a fair, trustworthy, and reliable Forex broker. You may be a great trader, but without a reliable and trustworthy broker, you will not be as successful as you should.

You may have an idea of what a Forex broker is, but it is important that we define who he is so that you have no doubt. A Forex broker can be defined as a company or firm that provides traders like you with access to a trading platform. As a trader, you need this platform to gain direct access to the Forex Market. Brokers are usually compensated via the bid-ask spreads of a given Forex currency pair.

The first step you should take is to search for reviews of the broker and find out what other traders think about him, his platform and services. Conducting due diligence is a must for any serious trader. You also need to check out the trading platform to find out if it matches your needs. Different traders have different needs when it comes to Forex trading so finding a right match is crucial.

Most Forex brokers will allow traders, who are possible clients, a chance to try out their platforms and test their services. They do this by offering a demo account. This provides traders with an excellent opportunity to try and understand how the system is like, how it functions and operates. As a trader, you need to try out as many platforms as possible so that you find one that you are quite happy and content with.

The Forex market operates 24 hours a day and sees a daily turnover more than $4 trillion. This makes it the world's largest financial market. As a trader, you will need some help navigating this market so your broker should be able to assist you as you trade on their platform.

Check for regulatory compliance

Most reputable Forex brokers are members of the NFA or National Futures Association and also registered with the US government as a commission merchant via the US Commodity Futures Trading Commission.

The NFA is an industry-wide body and self-regulating organization that covers the entire futures market in the USA. On the other hand, the CTFC is an independent government body that regulates the options markets and commodities futures markets in America.

Their aim is basically to protect the public as well as market users from manipulation.

A professionally looking website belonging to a Forex trader does not, in any way, guarantee that the broker is registered or regulated. Most of them will state that they are registered with the authorities and will display their registration details. You should never deposit your precious trading capital onto just any trading platform. Deal only with Forex brokers that are properly licensed and duly registered.

Proper Customer Service is Essential

Traders can access Forex markets at any time of day or night because the markets are accessible 24-hours each day. Your chosen broker should be available to provide you with essential services all the time. It should also be pretty simple to be able to access someone on phone for help. While chat-based service will do most of the time, there are instances when speaking to a real person will be of great assistance. Before signing up to any platform, consider making a quick call to customer service just so you get a feel for the quality of the customer service that they offer.

Check out the Currency Pairs Available

There are plenty of different currency pairs and even individual currencies out there. However, when it comes to Forex trading, only a couple of pairs are of any major importance. Some of the most useful Forex pairs include EUR/USD, GBP/USD, USD/CHF, and USD/JPY. Some top Forex brokers might offer a wider choice that may include the Chinese Yuan, the Hong Kong dollar, Australian dollar and so on. Always check out the list and ensure that the currency pairs you are interested in are available.

Checkout the Trading Portal

As a trader, you are connected directly to the Forex markets via the portal. It is therefore absolutely imperative that the portal is visually presentable and simple to use. You will be using this platform to practically carry out all the operations of your trades. Ensuring that it is in excellent working condition, easy to use, and reliable is something you must do. A good trading platform should come with essential buttons such as a simple sell or buy button. It should also come with an emergency button that allows traders to close all their open positions.

If the platform is poorly designed, then it will put your trades at huge risks. For instance, you could go short instead of long, or accidentally add to a given position instead of closing, and so on. Such mistakes will not only cost you money but also emotionally distressing. There are excellent options out there such as the Meta Trader which is among the most popular options among Forex traders.

While there is no perfect Forex broker in the world, identifying an excellent platform will allow you to focus more on your trades and technical analysis. You will then have more time to focus on developing appropriate trade strategies.

Significant Features of an Online Forex Broker

Every major Forex broker offers accounts with various features. These include some of the following.

Leverage and margin

As a trader, you will have access to a wide range of leverage amounts. These amounts will really depend on your Forex broker. Leverage could be 50:1, 100:1 and so on. The term leverage simply refers to a loan that you can access if you are a margin account holder. If you are an account holder and your account has a capital of $1000, then a Forex broker offering leverage of 50:1 will allow you to hold a position worth $50,000.

Leverage does work in favor of a trader especially when holding a winning position. The reason is that such a position stands a great chance of being profitable and making money. However, caution is needed because if a trade starts heading in the wrong direction, then the potential for losses is huge and could wipe out a trader's account. Therefore, caution is imperative whenever leverage is sought.

Spreads and Commissions

Online Forex brokers make their money mostly from spreads and commissions. Some opt for commissions which charge traders a certain percentage for accessing their platform. Sometimes the broker will charge based on the difference between the bid and ask price of a currency pair. Most traders prefer not to charge a commission but instead prefer to charge or make a commission from spreads. Generally, it is harder for a trader to make a profit on a wider spread. Common trading Forex pairs like the EUR/USD or GBP/USD have much tighter spreads compared to other pairs that may not be as tightly paired.

Forex brokers often offer first time traders or new clients a free amount which they can access and use to trade. Most Forex accounts are funded with very little money, sometimes as little as $50 or $100. However, this amount can greatly increase due to the offers and access to leverage power. This is among the reasons why Forex trading is so popular with first-time traders. As a new trader with a new account, you will have the option of opening either a mini, standard, or micro account. Each account has a minimum deposit requirement, so this is worth noting.

Ease of withdrawals and deposit

Generally, all major Forex brokers have their own policies when it comes to depositing and withdrawing your money. They also have things such as a funding policy and so on. A good broker will enable a variety of payment options including use of credit cards, direct payments from bank accounts or ACH, use of bank checks, wire transfers and also use of online payment processors like PayPal and others. Withdrawals from accounts are often processed via wire transfers or checks. Reputable brokers usually charge a processing fee during withdrawals. However, there is often no charge for making a deposit. You should check out these features before signing up with any broker.

2. Have Money Management Strategies

As a Forex trader, you will have to take risks with your capital. No strategy is 100% profitable, and even professional Forex traders lose money on some trades. The focus is always on the amount or percentage lost. Before entering any trade, you need to have a good strategy including the loss you are willing to incur before exiting a trade.

Most traders are willing to risk between 1% and 2% of their capital. Some are willing to get to 5%. However, the percentage you choose will largely depend on your risk appetite. There are a couple of things that you need to keep in mind though. When trading, the volumes could increase drastically, and this could have an effect on your capital. You will need to be flexible with some of your money management techniques when the time calls for it. This way, you will avoid losing money on your trades.

Some of the essential money management techniques that apply here include setting up your stop loss strategy. You need to decide exactly where to locate this important feature. The stop loss feature can be adjusted based on the current situation in the market as well as its volatility. It is only after the stop-loss process is complete that you will decide on the volumes of trade. Remember that money management is a crucial step and decisive part of any profitable trading strategy and should, therefore, not be overlooked but treated with the seriousness that it deserves.

3. The Right Trading Psychology

A successful trader has many admirable characteristics. These include the ability to determine stocks' direction and understanding a company's fundamentals. However, the single most crucial characteristic is the ability to exercise discipline and contain emotion.

Trading psychology

One of the most significant aspects of trading is the psychological aspect. Traders are often jumping in and out of trades on very short notices. Most of the time traders have to make very quick decisions with immense ramifications. A certain degree of calmness and presence of mind is therefore required. Emotions should never be allowed to cloud a trader's judgment or cause them to deviate from established trading plans.

The area of Forex trading is quite high paced with numerous possibilities and just as many pitfalls. Most of the time traders feel like the odds are stacked against them. Anytime a trader receives news about a certain currency, it is not uncommon to get scared. Sometimes they overreact and feel compelled to end a trade and other irrational acts. By so doing, a Forex trader may prevent losses but will also lose out on any possible profits.

Understanding fear

Traders need to understand what fear. This is a natural reaction to what a person perceives as a threat. Traders need to face up to this fear and see how they can get rid of it. Conquering fear is never easy and it does take some time and practice, but it is an essential aspect that needs to be tackled sooner rather than later. It is important for traders to isolate the single fear element, focus on it and try to isolate it as they trade. This is not as easy as it sounds, but it works eventually.

Greed is your Worst Enemy

On Wall Street, traders have an adage that says, "Pigs get slaughtered." This saying simply means that any greedy Forex traders will eventually lose out. Such traders tend to cling to a winning position and try to earn as much money out of it as possible.

Overcoming this negative emotion is never easy. This is because greed is based on a positive instinct that you can do better. However, getting just a little more out of a trade can cause a lot of trouble. This is why it is advisable to learn to keep emotions in check, to have a suitable trading plan and to determine the profitability and any losses on any given trade.

Chapter 6
Tips for Successful Forex Trading

Trading is more of an art than a science even though it is known for its ratios, charts, graphs, and numbers. Therefore, apart from learning the theory, you will need to hone your trading skills through regular practice and discipline. Keep doing self-analysis and test your trading plans to see how effective they are. There are essentially some steps which, if adhered to, will ensure that you trade safely and also make great profits.

A lot of undisciplined and inexperienced traders have incurred large losses over the years. You do not want to be like them. If you can determine the important steps and tips that will keep you safe and earn you money, then you will definitely be successful.

Never 100% Successful

It is a fact that no trader is ever successful 100% of the time. Many lose some of their trades but then they win big on other trades. Successful Forex trading is possible and can happen. However, you should not expect a 100% win rate. As a trader, you should endeavor to match up to the behavior and personality of the Forex markets. This means you should align your thoughts and practices to align with the Forex market and how it works and not the other way round. This is an absolutely crucial point. You should NOT endeavor to bend the market, so it becomes what you want it to be.

You can Succeed with 60% Wins or Lose with 80% Wins

Winning up to 80% of the trades you enter is absolutely phenomenal. A 0.8 win ratio is very respectable in the Forex world. However, you still lost 20% of the trades you entered which can be a little disappointing. Yet there are traders and trading systems that experience 60% wins or less. It is possible to be successful with only 45% wins.

Take the example of a trader who invests $1000 with the chance of winning $5000. Such a trader can afford to lose 4 trades because, with just one win, he will emerge $1000 richer. This is how it is possible to emerge a winner with less than 50% wins.

On the other hand, consider the trader who invests $5000 to win only $1000. This is a risky setup and the trader cannot afford to lose. The losses will be too costly. While this is just a demonstration, it shows how it is possible to lose over 50% of your trades and still emerge a winner.

Reduce your Overall Risk during Trading

There are plenty of factors that determine the outcome of a trade. As your skill level increases so will your ability to spot proper trade setups. Trading can be simple but is never easy. As a trader, you should endeavor to reduce your risks and exposure when trading in the foreign exchange markets. Here are some steps that you can take to keep yourself and your trades secure.

- **Start Trading with Small Amounts and Increase Organically**

One of the best tips that you can use is to start small. Do not load your account with a huge sum but try and start small. Use small amounts and low leverage. This is very important. You will be able to apply the skills you have learned and focus on trades without the fear of making huge losses. If you are to grow your account, then ensure that you grow your capital amount organically. This means let the capital grow from the returns of your trades and not loading your account from other sources.

- **Timing is Key so learn to be Patient**

As a trader, you really need to learn patience because it is an essential ingredient for success. One of the most important acts should be your opening trade. This is a crucial trade so you should give it your best analysis. You should also assess all other potential trades in good time. Make sure that you correctly time your market entry because the correct timing for this initial entry is crucial for success. For this, you will need to apply all your skills and knowledge about market trends and charting techniques. You should also ensure that you understand the entire process so that you are absolutely sure of what you are doing.

- **Learn the Limits of a Position before Entering**

    Every time you enter a trade, you must not only set your stop loss but also determine the maximum allowable loss that you are willing to take. The rules are pretty simple: Make sure you only risk money that you can afford o lose. Also, ensure that anytime you assess a position size and money required, there are sufficient funds for the trade. Avoid mixing cash meant for other projects with your trading capital.

    You also need to set a total loss limit at the close of each month. If at any one time during the month you get to this limit, then trading should cease and you should wait for the following month. Also, should your losses consistently exceed your income, then you should probably cease trading and take a step back. Take time to reassess your strategies, revamp your technical skills, and trading fundamentals. Also, have a journal of all your trades so that you review them and take note of where it is that you are going wrong. Should you go back to trading and start making profits, put aside some funds just in case anything goes wrong. Such setbacks should be mitigated with the funds you set aside.

- **Remember to be Diligent and with your Trading Plan**

    As a Forex trader, you will enjoy success when you eventually learn to balance hard work such as chart analysis with sound judgments and lots of patience. Too many traders often give up on their trades without giving them sufficient time to run their course. This is why a majority of first time traders and investors eventually give up and quit. To be a winner, you should learn patience, stick to your plan and do not quit.

How to Determine the most Suitable Trading Strategy

There are many Forex traders out there who spend years implementing trading strategies that do not match them. This can be disastrous because the chances of success are very low. It is important to make some considerations before embarking on trading using a particular strategy. Here are some useful points that you should consider. When you take these points into consideration, then you are likely to save yourself a lot of hurt, pain, time, effort, and money.

1. Determine if you desire a regular income or grow wealth

First, let us understand the difference between earning an income from trade and growing wealth. If you trade Forex to earn an income, then you probably target to earn a certain amount each month for your own personal use. However, when you want to grow wealth, you aim to grow your amount by a certain percentage each year.

Trading for an income

If you want to trade Forex to earn a monthly or weekly income, then you need to identify trades that occur within a short period of time. It also means that you should spend more hours on the trading platform. Some of the options you have regarding trade strategies include short-term swing trading, day trading, and scalping.

Trading to grow wealth

You can choose to have fewer trading options when you want to grow your wealth. This essentially allows you to spend fewer hours on the trading platform by choosing trades with higher timeframes. Some of the trading options you can choose include position trading and swing trading.

2. Determine the amount of time you have

You need to decide how much time you can dedicate to Forex trading each day and each week. People with a fulltime job and those who cannot put in 12-hour days should consider Forex strategies that do not require a lot of time investment such as position trading and swing trading.

Forex trade strategies like scalping, day trading and all other short-term trading strategies are for traders with all the time in the world. Therefore, choose any of these strategies if you enjoy them.

3. Find out if a particular strategy suits you

There are a good number of Forex trading strategies out there. All these can be split into two distinct categories. These are high win strategies with low reward: risk ratios and the low win rate with high reward: risk ratio.

You need to determine which of these two approaches suits you best. Apparently, they can both make you money as they are both profitable. Therefore, you need to determine which of these two categories you are more comfortable with.

Do you wish to take huge risks for high returns or are you comfortable playing it safe with low-risk trades? Swing trading, for instance, has a high chance for success but with low returns. On the other hand, position trading has lower win rates with much larger gains.

Summary

In short, therefore, we can conclude the following:

Swing trading: This strategy can be used for wealth creation or income generation. It is suitable for traders who can only spare a couple of hours each day to trade.

Day trading: This strategy is more popular with traders seeking to generate a regular income. It requires a Forex trader who has time on their hands and can spend long stretches of time in front of a screen.

Position trading: This is more of a wealth building strategy and is best suited for traders who do not have a lot of time on their hands. Such people often have another job or occupation elsewhere.

Before you embark on learning about any of these Forex trading strategies, you should first make the following determinations.

- What trading goals do you have?
- How much time do you have available?
- Does a particular strategy or approach suit your personality?

Only when you can address these concerns should you then proceed to start trading.

Conclusion

Thanks for making it through to the end of this book, let's hope it was informative and able to provide you with all of the tools you need to achieve your goals whatever they may be.

The next step you need to take is to apply all the useful lessons you have learned from this book. Remember that all the theory, technical analysis, availability of funds and so on, will not help you much if you lack discipline or proper understanding of when to enter and exit trades.

Another important factor that a successful Forex trader needs to keep in mind is that they need to be disciplined and not let emotions cloud their trades. Too many young or green traders lose money while trading simply due to lack of discipline or letting emotions get the best of them.

Finally, if you found this book useful in any way, a review on Amazon is always appreciated!

www.ingramcontent.com/pod-product-compliance
Lightning Source LLC
Chambersburg PA
CBHW030035230526
45472CB00002B/529